Caroline's Secret

LATTER-DAY DAUGHTERS

BOOKS IN THE LATTER-DAY DAUGHTERS SERIES

1832 Maren's Hope
1838 Laurel's Flight
1840 Hannah's Treasure
1844 Anna's Gift
1846 Catherine's Remembrance
1856 Clarissa's Crossing
1859 Janey's Own
1862 Violet's Garden
1878 Caroline's Secret
1896 Esther's Celebration
1897 Ellie's Gold
1910 Sarah's Quest
1918 Gracie's Angel
1978 Marciea's Melody

Caroline's Secret

LATTER-DAY DAUGHTERS

Carol Lynch Williams

Published by
Deseret Book Company
Salt Lake City, Utah

*To the Primary-age children of the Mapleton Eighth Ward
and to Steve and Wendy Rogers, the best neighbors
a person could ask for*

© 1997 Carol Lynch Williams

All rights reserved. No part of this book may be reproduced in any form or by any means without permission in writing from the publisher, Deseret Book Company, P.O. Box 30178, Salt Lake City, Utah 84130. This work is not an official publication of The Church of Jesus Christ of Latter-day Saints. The views expressed herein are the responsibility of the author and do not necessarily represent the position of the Church or of Deseret Book Company.

Deseret Book and Cinnamon Tree are registered trademarks of Deseret Book Company.

Library of Congress Cataloging-in-Publication Data

Williams, Carol Lynch.
  Caroline's secret / by Carol Lynch Williams.
    p. cm. — (The Latter-day daughters series)
  Summary: Living with her Mormon family in Farmington, Utah, in 1878, thirteen-year-old Caroline hears a secret which causes her to change her mind about wanting to become a famous spy.
  ISBN 1-57345-318-8 (pbk.)
  [1. Spies—Fiction. 2. Mormons—Fiction. 3. Family life—Utah—Fiction. 4. Utah—Fiction.] I. Title. II. Series.
PZ7.W65588Car   1997
[Fic]—dc21   97-39829
                                                                          CIP
                                                                           AC

Printed in the United States of America   8006

10 9 8 7 6 5 4 3 2 1

"We expect to see a radical change, a reformation in the midst of this people."

Brigham Young, 1877
Address given at organization of Davis Stake

Contents

Chapter 1
The Spy and the Fire 1

Chapter 2
Peeking In on Mama 12

Chapter 3
Waiting for Father 22

Chapter 4
Time with Father 30

Chapter 5
Talking to Joshua 41

Chapter 6
Wagon Ride 52

Chapter 7
Caught . . . Again 62

Chapter 8
The First Meeting for Children 71

Chapter 9
A Secret for My Heart Only 78

Glossary
In Caroline's Own Words 83

What Really Happened 85

Chapter One

The Spy and the Fire

From where I sat, no one could see me. I'd done it on purpose. Hidden myself, I mean. No spy places herself right in the view of the people she's spying on. Not according to the books I've read in Father's store. And anyway, from where I was perched like a bird on a limb, I could see everything: the whole of the yard here in the back, including the apricot trees, the outhouse, and a bit of the barn. I could see the wide, open field, yellow from heat. And the Rogers family's cow. A few chickens. And both boys. It was *what* those two boys were doing that wasn't quite clear.

See the glossary at the end of this book for an explanation of unusual words and expressions marked with an asterisk (*).

"Don't go on shoving me like that," Peter said.

"I wasn't shoving," Joshua answered.

I could see straight enough that Joshua was only jostling Peter a slight bit. And not enough to matter at all, either. But Peter is a baby, and that's the real truth. No matter that he's a year older than me. Fourteen on a boy is wasted years.

I was hot. Sweat beaded up on my forehead and a little trickled down the side of my face. You'd think sitting in the shade of a tree would have made me feel cooler, but it wasn't so. The branches seemed to hold the heat close to my body. Not a lick of wind was moving, and the sun beat down so that even in this tree it somehow managed to squeeze past needles and sit on me some. And the air . . . it was so thick and heavy it practically had to be chewed first before you could breathe any of it in.

"What if you get caught?" Joshua asked.

A bit of smoke went up between Peter and Joshua, a soft curl, one so unnoticeable that only a famous spy, someone like me or Jesse Parker, would have even caught a glimpse. Jesse Parker is the man in Father's books. I'm learning all I can about being a spy from him.

Smoke grew a little thicker, and then I knew.

Why, those two scoundrels were making a fire! And after Mama made it clear as stream water that Peter was to stay away from anything dangerous like that.

"Mama's out visiting," Peter said. "She left Caroline here to keep an eye on the place. And anyway, we're far enough from the house that nobody will see and still close enough that I'll hear the buggy when Mama gets back."

An ugly look went across Joshua's face. "That sister of yours is a batch of trouble," he said.

"Why are you telling me what I already know?" Peter asked.

My blood began to boil, and it had nothing to do with the heat of the day. That ol' Peter. Here he was, the near baby of the family, turning on me.

"I don't know how you can stand a sister like that," Joshua said. "Always running to tattle on you." Joshua spit into the yellow grass.

"She's spoiled," Peter said. Just like that. Like

it was a fact or something that should be written down as such.

I felt my eyes grow big, but being the spy that I was, I didn't say a word. I sure wanted to. I wanted to get right down there between the two of them and step on their fire and their nasty, traitorous words.

"Forget about her," Peter said. "Let's get this going. I want to conduct an experiment and I can't, for sure, while Mama's home. She'd take the hide off me for disobeying her strict command."

Joshua didn't work on the fire. He sat back on his feet and looked toward the tree where I hid. I felt myself freeze up despite the terrible heat. It seemed as if Joshua stared straight at me. Perhaps the dark green of my dress didn't hide me after all. Perhaps he saw my yellow hair, though I'd tucked it up under a blue kerchief the best I could.

"Well, she's an ugly little thing," Joshua said. "Skinny and knobby where it seems she should be soft and round. Now, think of Marie. Marie is soft-looking."

Peter sat back, too. "I should say. There's two Maries to one Caroline."

Ugly? I thought. *Skinny? Knobby? Why, that Joshua Walker. That . . . that . . .* I couldn't think of a word bad enough (that I was allowed to say) that would fit him. Anger ran through me thicker than the air. And then sadness. I felt tears burn hot into my eyes.

"I said let's not think about her anymore," Peter said. "If I didn't know better, I'd say you are sweet on Caroline."

Joshua fell backwards. His feet shook at the sky as if he kicked out a warning. His body jerked like he was having a fit, and he moved his head this way and that.

Your dying scene is taking way too long, I wanted to shout out. But of course I couldn't.

Joshua flopped over on his stomach and flapped his arms like he was getting ready to fly away. From where I sat, I could see dirt and grass pieces hanging onto his hair. *Serves him right to get so dirty,* I thought. Then Joshua went all limp, like he was dead.

"Finally," I said, breathing the word out.

Peter had watched Joshua's whole dance with a big, fat grin across his face. Suddenly he threw himself backwards and started gyrating* on the ground, too. "Boys," I said under my breath. I closed my eyes and shook my head a bit. When I looked at the two of them again, they were slumped over each other, laughing.

I looked away and swallowed. There was a bit of a lump in my throat caused by Joshua's words. Why, I'd thought him different, that was all. When no one was around, Joshua had been nice to me. I wiped at the tears that were starting to spill from my eyes. He was the worst traitor of them all.

"We've got to hurry and get this fire a-going," Peter said after a moment. He and Joshua bent over their work.

"Blow a bit more," Peter said. Joshua crowded close and I couldn't quite see what happened.

The two of them worked hard for a minute and I had a chance to stretch out my mind and remember a few days before. I'd been coming back from the store, and Joshua had caught up with me and walked me home. He'd been so nice that afternoon. He'd talked to me the whole way and never let on once that he thought I was ugly.

Or too skinny. I bit my bottom lip, hoping I could forget the painful words Joshua had said about me. But I couldn't. Once a saying gets into my mind, I can't forget it. Mama says it's because memories and words stick to me like flies in honey.

I saw the flame then, starting up tiny, pretty as it could be. It seemed to come to life, dancing and moving, pulling up a bit, then curling down.

I forced myself to concentrate on my spying. "Now why would those two naughties want to start a fire on a day as hot as this?" I said to myself, only I said it so all I could really hear was my breath and my lips smacking together. Spies have to keep quiet.

Peter and Joshua, Traitor Joshua, sat as close as they could to the flame, like they wanted to roast their own faces.

Peter had said something about an experiment, but I was pretty sure it was nothing he'd learned in school.

"Look at it," Peter said, and Traitor Joshua leaned back because the flames were growing taller and eating up the ground near the two of them.

"What's your experiment?" Traitor Joshua asked.

"Different colors," Peter said, but he didn't move. It seemed he was hypnotized by the flames and couldn't free himself.

"What?" the traitor asked.

A slight breeze came up then, one I could barely even feel, and pushed the fire west a bit, toward Papa's grainfield that stood golden in the heat.

And then, like a bat screeching from a cave, Mama swooped down from out of nowhere carrying a wet sack. I hadn't even seen her coming.

"Thwack," said the bag, wrapping itself around Peter's left arm.

Then *thwack* again. The bag left a wet mark on the traitor's back. Both noises caused me to jump, and for a moment I teetered on my limb and had to hang on for dear life. My heart pounded a mile a minute. Mama sure had surprised me—and those two rotten boys as well.

They crouched near the ground as Mama beat at the flames that were only knee-high.

"What in . . . ," *thwack,* "the world . . . ," *thwack,* "are you . . . ," *thwack,* "two thinking . . . ," *thwack,* "about?" Mama kept beating at the fire with the wet sack. In a second she had it under control, and then out completely. All that was left was a black path between Peter and Traitor Joshua, who both cowered and simpered* like maybe their silly expressions could save them from Mama's wrath.

"Stand up, you two," Mama said, and she helped the boys to their feet by tugging at their ears.

"Ow, ow, Mama," Peter said, and I could see he meant it. But Joshua didn't say anything at all, though his face wore a hurt expression.

"Don't you know what you almost did?" Mama shouted. Mama rarely shouts. In fact, as good as my memory is, I can only remember her shouting once, and that was when my baby brother drowned.

"Well," Peter said, "I was thinking about . . ."

He sure struggled to find words. A smile

spread across my face, warm enough to almost make me feel better.

Mama's face was as red as some of the flames had been. Her dark hair was loose and curled near her cheeks. I noticed, like any good spy would, that her apron was splotched with water and soot.

"You could have burned this whole valley," Mama said. "You could have burned your father's wheat field."

"I'm sorry, Mama," Peter said, and he hung his head.

"And you," Mama said, pointing hard at Joshua. "Was this foolish prank your idea?"

Joshua shook his head and opened his mouth, but not a word came out.

"Get on back to the house," Mama said, her voice low and dangerous sounding. She stepped toward Peter and Joshua and moved the wet feed sack like it was a weapon. I would have giggled then, but the three of them were right near my hiding place, and as any good spy knows, as Jesse Parker knows, when someone is near your hiding place, this is the best time to keep quiet.

Caroline's Secret

"Caroline," Mama said. "Get out of that tree. I'd prefer you'd act like a lady."

I felt my skin go from warm to cool to burning hot at being found out in front of Joshua, but I made my way down the tree, using the limbs as steps.

"Why, Caroline was around that whole time," Joshua said. But Mama put a quick stop to his words with a snap of the wet bag.

CHAPTER TWO

Peeking In on Mama

Mama wouldn't take any excuses from my brother. Or from his best friend and my worst enemy, Joshua. She sent the latter home with these words ringing in his ears: "*And* Mr. Walker, if I ever catch you playing with fire in my yard again, I'll send your skin back to your family and they'll have to stuff you so the wind won't blow you away." Mama has never been one to watch what comes out of her mouth too close.

Then she turned on Peter. She wrung him out good, like an old dishcloth, I have to admit.

"Young man," Mama's voice was low and deadly sounding. It made the hairs stand up on my arms, even in the heat of the day.

Peter could hardly move, though you wouldn't know it if you weren't as good a spy as I am. I was peeking through the crack in the front room door, watching the whole thing. I saw his body go all stiff. He was scared plenty.

Mama didn't say anything for one long minute. Peter moved, uncomfortable in her silence. I could tell by the way he kept swallowing that he wanted to loosen his collar.

"Young man," Mama said again.

This is gonna be one lengthy lecture, I thought. Of course, I didn't say it or I would have been standing right there alongside Peter. Not even the bravest of spies would want that punishment from Florence Gallagher. It's worse than torture, I know that for a fact.

"Do you realize," Mama started and she stretched her words out so that it took her about fifteen seconds to even say *realize*. She has a talent for drawing out words. "When the last time we had rain was?"

Peter acted like he was thinking about when the last time we had rain was, but I really think he was figuring a way out of the front room. I mean, that's what I would have been doing.

"Do you recall the day?" Mama asked. Now

she was speaking fast, like someone had wound her up tight. My mama has a talent for speaking fast, too. "In the late spring when the rain last fell? Do you recall how I told you to clean out the barrels to catch that falling gift from heaven? Do  you recall that you didn't really want to do what I asked? Your father was home and he helped you that morning. Do you recall that he very nearly caught his death of a cold? And I said to you, I remember it exactly, and so do you, Peter, I said to you, 'Son, we'll be needing that water, you mark my words.'" Mama rocked back on her heels. This whole speech had taken her fifteen seconds, also. My mama is a talented woman, and if I weren't going to be the only female spy in all the state of Deseret,* I do think I'd be a questioner like her.

Peter was silent. Watching his face was like watching someone on the stage. First he looked puzzled, thinking about the last rain, then perplexed* at Father's having to help Thomas and him make sure the rain barrels were cleaned out, then sad at Father's having caught his near death of a cold, then slightly surprised at Mama's prophecy. He was acting his part real good, if I do say so myself.

"I'm waiting for an answer, Peter," Mama said.

"I remember it all, Mama," Peter said.

"Why?" Mama said and she drew out the word about four counts.

Peter hesitated. I could tell by his face that he wasn't sure if he should answer or not. "I remember because you've just reminded me," he said at last.

Mama turned from Peter until she was facing me just about eyeball to eyeball. Her mouth twitched some and I could see she was trying not to smile. I didn't move a muscle. I don't even think my heart beat for those few seconds Mama stared at my listening-in place. She turned back to face my brother. "That question was not meant for you to answer, Peter," she said.

"Sorry, Mama," Peter said and bowed his head a bit. Yessiree, he was playing his part just fine.

Mama took in a deep breath, then walked over to Peter. She reached for him, and as she did, he was hidden from me. Mama is a tall and stately woman, I've heard others say this is so.

"A fire could have destroyed everything we have, Peter Gallagher. Everything."

Peter's arms went around Mama. He hugged onto her tight. "I'm sorry," he said, and I could tell by his voice he meant every word of what he was saying. "I am, Mama."

"Son, why would you do such an evil thing?"

"It was an experiment, Mama," Peter said, his voice muffled in Mama's girth.* "On the different colors of fire."

I moved away from my listening-in place, my mouth opened wide. Why, my brother was hugging Mama. Wouldn't Joshua be surprised to know that? I spied in on Mama and Peter again.

Mama took him by the shoulders and then bent a bit at the waist till she was staring my brother right in the eyes. "This is no time of year for experiments," she said, and Peter nodded.

Mama straightened herself up tall. "Caroline," she called. I froze for a second there in the hallway. Then I thawed out quick and moved as fast and light-footed as I could away from the door, trying to get down the hall and into the kitchen where I was supposed to be peeling potatoes. I didn't make it.

The double doors opened wide. Both Mama and Peter came out. "To your chores now," she said, and he was off like a rabbit.

"Into the kitchen, Caroline," Mama said. "We've dinner to make and the Sabbath to prepare for."

I beat Mama into the kitchen by one step, but there was no way she was not going to notice the potatoes weren't peeled. I went to my pan and pulled out a paring knife.

"I can't believe you did that, Caroline," Mama said.

Caught! I was caught spying—caught like a fox in one of Father's traps.

"I cannot believe that you would let your brother and that no-good friend of his start a fire on our property."

Relief went through me like cold water. I hadn't been caught! Then I stopped. I wasn't to blame for their doings. My mouth dropped open wide enough for someone to drive a wagon through.

"Mama," I started, but she didn't let me finish.

"I trusted you."

"But . . . ," I said.

"I left the welfare of this household in your hands," she said.

"Well . . . ," I said.

"A fire would have taken out this entire valley. It's as dry as a bone out there."

"I . . . ," I said.

"When your father finds out . . ." Mama turned her back on me then and started the work of flouring up pork steaks for frying.

I reached for a potato and washed the dried earth from it. That was the worst thing Mama could say. To me, Father is perfect, standing right up there in righteousness alongside Brother Brigham Young, only with a much happier-looking face. Probably because he only has two wives, while our dear prophet has twenty. At least that's what I've heard rumored. About Father's happiness, I mean.

"You're not planning on talking to Father, are

you?" I asked, a funny feeling running clear through me to my fingertips.

"Perhaps I will," Mama said.

I edged up close to her, a wet potato in one hand. "I tell you I didn't know about the fire hardly at all," I said.

"You were sitting pretty up in the tree. Why, all the neighbors could see you there."

"They could?" I asked, surprised now. I had thought that a rather good hiding place.

Mama nodded, flour covering the fingers of one hand.

"It embarrasses me some to think I have a thirteen-year-old daughter who listens in on others' conversations *and* climbs trees."

I blinked. Somehow I had to try and change the conversation around now. And quick, too. I could hear a lecture boiling up on the back of Mama's tongue. "Mama," I said, and I moved over and started to peel fast, "I didn't burn down the valley, or even our properties, with my listening." I wanted to tell her all the terrible things that were said about me, but I knew that would only add fuel to the flame. If I hadn't been listening in, peeking in, eavesdropping on private conversations, I would have never heard those things. I kept my mouth closed tight except to say, "I did no real harm."

Mama nodded. Her dark red hair was up now, neat as it had been before the fire. "Don't try and move me from the path I'm taking, Caroline," she said.

"Mama." My voice somehow came out all long-sounding. I sliced a potato into a pan of cold water.

"And don't whine at me. All I need to put me in my grave is to know that I have a whining, spying, tree-climbing child."

I turned to face Mama. "I was only doing what you told me to do," I said.

"I never told you to climb a tree." Mama didn't even look up from her work.

"You did tell me to keep an eye on the two of those boys," I said. "And that's not the easiest of all tasks. They hate me, I'll have you know. So in order to catch them at whatever they were doing, I had to spy." A lump came up in my throat as big as the potato I was holding onto. I didn't care if Peter hated me, because I knew that deep down in his old heart he and I would be friends just because we are family. But it bothered me that Joshua was such a traitor. And after all his kind words to my face. My eyes stung from hot tears.

Mama glanced back and, seeing my face, came at me with floury hands and a pork steak.

"Is my baby girl about to cry?" she asked in a startled way, and then she wrapped her arms around me.

I nodded my head in her big bosom. The buttons on the front of her dress scratched at my skin, but it was a comfortable scratching. Then I shook my head no. *No! I wasn't going to cry,* I thought, tucked safe in Mama's arms, her warm smell filling me. No! I wasn't gonna cry because of some boy.

Mama kissed the top of my head. "Get back to work," she said. "Your father will be here soon."

I went on peeling, my stomach flopping between the good feelings of my dear father coming home and the awful feelings that Joshua Walker hated me.

CHAPTER THREE

Waiting for Father

Father came home before the bread was crusty brown on top.

When he is home, our house feels like the sun's come to visit. I get that feeling all over me: goodness. I want to do good and feel good and be good clear down to the tiniest part of my heart. Father does that to people. To nearly everyone, I think. Of course, I can't be too sure about the way other people are feeling. Even a spy can't look on the heart of man, only God can, that's what Father's always saying. But I can see people's faces when he's around. They look as happy as I feel when I'm with him, so that is how I have arrived at this conclusion.*

"He's home. Early," Mama said, looking up

with surprise from the platter she'd been putting the fried pork steaks on. She set aside her big fork and came close to dropping all of dinner to the floor. She grabbed at an old cloth and wiped her hands, then went off at quite a fast pace. "I'll just tidy myself a bit," she said as she left the room. "Caroline, you see to things being put out nicely on the table." And she was gone.

There's a bit of truth I need to say right here, and that is that somehow my mama knows when Father is close by. I'm not too sure how she does it, but she has yet to be wrong. Perhaps she has a bit of spy blood running through her veins. I know Mama would never admit to this, but the thought that I was like Mama in this way made me feel happy inside.

"How does she do it?" I said to no one. "How does she know when he's close?"

I listened hard to see if maybe I could hear what Mama must have heard to alert her to Father being near, but there wasn't a thing but the sound of children's voices. And those came from a distance.

I moved around the kitchen, setting things

out as nice as I could: the platter of pork steaks, covered with a cloth to keep away the flies, the dish of beans, dried apples made into a pie, the potatoes that I had fried just a little too much, and the bread a tiny bit too pale. Next to the bread I set out a dish of butter Mama had molded into a rose shape. Butter fit for company—or for Father's first night home in two weeks. The good smells of all this food mingled together caused my mouth to start watering. Now all I needed was to get the milk.

"Father," I heard Peter call out, and my stomach leaped so hard I'm sure I felt it knocking at my back teeth. "I've done all you asked, taken care of things just the way you said."

I put the plates, Mama's good china, out on the table, placing cups upside down in the center of each one. Then I laid a knife and fork near the right side of each person's place and set out napkins Mama had made herself not long after we arrived here in Farmington.*

And then Mama was back in the kitchen. "He always surprises me," she said.

I glanced over at her. She wasn't really talking to me, but voicing her feelings to the warm air of the kitchen. I saw that her cheeks were pink, more from excitement than from the heat of the day or the work of preparing a meal. Her hair was done up real nice and her clothes were changed for this happy dinner and the time she would have with Father.

"He's close now," I said. Voices told me that. I could hear Peter, plain as day, and Marie, too, both talking at Father, trying to make him hear all that was important to them, I suppose. Marie really should have been in here with Mama and me, working in the kitchen. Soft, round Marie, my beautiful older sister. For a moment, I resented her being free from chores and walking with Father.

But the thought of him made my bad feelings slip away. Until I heard Peter's voice again.

"You won't need to listen to any of Caroline's tall tales, Father," he said. "Not about my behavior. You know how she exaggerates anyway."

"Does she?" Father asked, and both Peter and

Marie laughed, though Peter didn't seem to be putting his heart into his chuckles.

Peter. I gritted my teeth at his words. Well, I could just gamble (though I never really would, being that it's a sin) that he wasn't telling Father *all* of his adventures. And he even had the gall* to try and make Father not listen to me. As if I would even let one word of his terrible behavior ruin this evening. Anyway, there was evidence enough in the yard. Evidence even Peter would have a hard time explaining: the black spot where the fire had burned only a few hours earlier. If I was lucky, there might be a little smoke left.

"Run and freshen up, Caroline," Mama said, looking past me to where Father would be entering the house.

"Yes ma'am," I said.

"And thank you for all your help."

I looked at Mama, all new for Father, rosy-colored and pretty, and noticed she was trembling. Mama's hands were shaking just a bit. Why, she was nervous to see Father again!

I started out of the room and made my way

up the stairs, running my hand along the wall as I went.

Was Mama so in love that she trembled at the thought of Father home? This idea made me wonder. Not because Father isn't wonderful—he is. But the two of them have been married what seems an eternity already. Is that what marriage would be for me? If so, this was a secret as good as any spy could expect.

In my room I poured a fresh basin of water, cool from the pump, and began to wash at my face, then neck and hands, in the order Mama had taught me. At the mirror I looked hard at myself.

My mind jumped all of a sudden to Joshua. For a moment I saw his dark hair shining in the day's sunlight, looking more brown than black. I could see his eyes, blue like the sky in the early morning. He had freckles, and he was slender and a good deal taller than Peter.

I leaned close to the mirror, feeling almost like I could see Joshua standing there beside me, his reflection right close to mine.

I closed my eyes and tried to imagine his voice.

Coming clear to my mind, clear and fresh and cold as new snow, were his hateful words all over again: "She's an ugly little thing. Skinny and knobby where it seems she should be soft and round."

"No!" I said, opening my eyes. "I won't remember!"

"Ugly little thing." The words seemed to float around my head, more annoying than mosquitoes or gnats.

And he had been so nice to me before. He had walked me home and spoken to me kindly.

"Don't think about it," I said to my reflection. "Boys are cruel." This was something I had overheard Sister Mangelson say once when she found her largest melon stolen from her garden. I had been listening in at her window and heard her say those very words to Mama when she inquired if Peter had come across a melon himself.

"Joshua is cruel," I said. The words I spoke now stung my heart the same as the things I had heard him say about me earlier.

Father's voice came booming up the stairs

then. "Sweet Caroline. I've been gone two whole weeks. Come kiss me hello."

"Father," I said to my reflection. I dabbed at my eyes with the sleeve of my green dress till the tears that had appeared were gone.

"I don't need to feel sweet about Joshua Walker," I said to myself, checking one last time to see that my hair was neat. "There is nothing wrong with dying an old maid. I have a mission before me. I'll continue being a spy and make that my life's work."

Then I ran out the door and down the stairs to see Father, feeling broken-hearted at my lonesome plight.

Chapter Four

Time with Father

Each time Father is home there is cause to celebrate. That's what Mama says, and I agree. Mama always makes his favorite foods, and two days before his arrival we clean the house from top to bottom.

Our home is beautiful because of Father, of course. It is a large two-story building made from adobe (to keep it cool) and granite (to make it look pretty). And it does—look pretty, I mean. Sometimes, when the sun catches it just right, it shines like diamonds must when they're linked together with gold on a necklace.

Father brings happiness in with him, just like he built it into our home, carefully and with lots of space. Maybe that doesn't make much sense, happiness having lots of space, but I can explain. It's like this one time when I saw the first of our sheep give birth to a tiny lamb.  The baby, once it was cleaned up some, appeared to be as sweet as the juice in a clover blossom. And watching it try to stand filled me with so much joy that it seemed to expand my heart some. That's what I mean. Pure happiness sure can make your heart feel wide open.

Dinner was leisurely, and then Father and Mama visited in the parlor, talking in low voices, while Peter went to the chores and Marie and I cleaned up the dishes and put food away.

"What a wonderful, marvelous day," Marie said with a sigh like a breath of canyon wind. She washed at the dishes like she wasn't really thinking about what she was doing.

"Well, it's better now that Father's home," I said. "You missed a spot." I handed the plate back to her so she could go over it again with the rag.

Marie took the plate and smiled at nothing but the thin air.

I leaned toward her. "I said, it's better now that Father is home."

Marie nodded, then pursed her lips and smiled again. "What a glorious day."

I raised my eyebrows. Marie had been on a picnic with some of her friends from school. Picnics are fun, I suppose, but not so much fun as to cause Marie to act like this. She wasn't listening to a thing I said. If she were, then she could have heard the sorrow in my voice. And a girl of sixteen really should listen to her younger sister when she's troubled. At least that's the way I see it.

"Peter," I began, "had company today."

Marie rinsed the dish she held, then tried to catch her reflection in the shininess the water left behind. She said nothing, only smiled at herself.

"You're lagging," I said. "I want to visit with Father. Do hurry."

Marie began washing again and then started humming a song with no real tune. At least not when Marie sang it. Who knows what song she was after?

I heaved a sigh and slapped my drying cloth

around in the air like I was aiming to knock down a pesky fly. "You're probably wondering who."

"Who?" Marie echoed.

"Who came to visit." I didn't give Marie time to guess but raced ahead. Not that I was worried she'd interrupt, the way she was acting now. I just needed someone to talk to, to share my bruised heart with. "It was Joshua Walker."

Marie looked me at wide-eyed. "Michael Walker," she said.

"No, not Michael. His younger brother. Joshua."

Marie looked at me straight in the eye then. She moved forward until our noses almost touched. Her eyes, the same green color that mine are, seemed to shine. "Caroline," she said and she reached out with a wet hand and placed it on my shoulder.

"You'll leave a print," I said.

"I'm sorry," Marie said, removing her hand, but she didn't look a bit sorry. "The Walkers are a family strong in the gospel."

"What?"

"And pure in heart."

"Huh?"

"A family firm in the truth."

"Why," I said, having to gasp for breath, "why, Joshua is truly rotten to his core. He said the meanest things to me today."

"Did he? How you do spin a yarn, Caroline."

"Marie, are you even listening?"

"You said Joshua was rotten."

"He is."

"You said he was rotten to the core."

"And I'm sincere. I mean it."

Marie began to wash the dishes with a fury. "His brother Michael is working on the new hotel."

I shrugged my shoulders. "What's that have to do with Joshua being awful to me?"

"Perhaps you imagined it."

"What?" I said in a loud voice.

"Girls," called Mama. "Are you finished?"

"Yes, ma'am," said Marie. And so did I.

"Marie, look me over good, from top to bottom," I said.

"Whatever for?"

"Please," I said. "I need to know something."

Marie rinsed the last of the dishes, then turned to me before she went to wipe down the table. I stood as tall as I could, trying to look as plump as possible. There was nothing I could do about the ugly part.

"Yes?"

"How do I look to you?"

Marie cocked her head to the side like I've seen birds do and ran her eyes over me.

I felt my face color, but I kept still, fidgeting only a little with my drying cloth.

"You look a lot like I did three years ago," Marie said at last. "Mama says you and I take after Father's side of the family. Funny, that the two girls would take after their father and the only boy who lived would look so much like his mother."

"But am I skinny? Am I knobby?" These were hard words to force from my mouth, but I had to know.

Marie moved her head to the other side. "No more than any other thirteen-year-old girl." Then she hurried on with the kitchen work until there was nothing left for me to do but put away the dried dishes.

We had family time that night, like we always do when Father comes home. Marie played the organ and Mama sang with a voice as sweet as birds in the summer. Father joined in, his voice deep and full. I sing on key, but I'd rather be spying or snuggling close to Father. Still, I did my duty as a daughter and joined in on the harmony. Peter, though he doesn't look it, can sing fine, too. And sing he did. Too soon it was time for bed.

"Father, I need to speak with you," I said, before I headed to my room upstairs. I was feeling especially knobby and I didn't think I could take any more of Marie's wistful looks or smiles that seemed to erupt for no reason. "Do you have a moment?"

"There's always time for you, Caroline," Father said, and I was warmed to my very heart by his words.

Mama sat in her rocker, knitting. Father says there is not a faster knitter in all the country of Deseret, and I do believe him. Father says that he thinks Mama could keep all the Saints supplied in stockings if she had the wool available. I'm not so sure this is a fact, but Mama laughs when he says it.

I went and sat next to Father on the settee,* then gathered in all the breath I had, so I'd have courage to speak. "I've missed you very much, Father," I said.

He nodded and smiled at me, then smoothed my hair a little with his large hand.

"You know you can visit at any time. I am only a few blocks away."

Father married Mama's very best friend, Sister Elizabeth, two years ago. They have no children together, something Mama calls a burden for Sister Elizabeth.

"First, no husband," Mama sometimes says. "And now no children." She always shakes her head sad and sorrowful, as if to say children are wonderful. It's obvious she hasn't peered too close at her own son, Peter, or she'd be congratulating Sister Elizabeth on her barrenness.

"I know I can visit," I said. "But I like having you here at home."

"Sister Elizabeth would see you anytime,"

Mama said from her rocker. Her knitting needles flashed in the early evening light.

"Or you could come and visit me at the store," Father said.

I knew this to be true, but I didn't say anything about it. Instead, in a rush of words I blurted out, "Father, do you think I'm ugly?" I hadn't meant for the words to come out sounding so full of hate, but they did. Feelings left over from earlier, I guess.

"What?" Father asked, and I could tell by his voice that he was puzzled at my question.

"I heard it said that people think I'm ugly," I said.

"And how did you hear such a thing?" Mama asked. Her knitting needles took on a dangerous glimmer.

"Uh," I said, knowing full well Mama was going to ask if I had gotten this information while spying.

"Were you peeking in on another private conversation?"

I bowed my head. Then I nodded. I was ashamed. Not only had I let out these hurtful words, opening my soul up, but I'd also been caught, again, as a spy.

Father put his finger beneath my chin and raised my head. "Caroline," he said in a voice most sincere. "I think you are the most beautiful thirteen-year-old I know. You look much the way my mother did when she was younger. You've seen the sketches my father did when they were first married."

I *had* seen those pictures. Some were framed and scattered about the house. Others were in a book of sketches. Grandfather had thought Grandmother beautiful. All of his drawings said so.

I looked at the portrait on the wall near the fireplace. "She doesn't look knobby," I said.

"What?" Mama asked. Her voice went squeaky at the end and the knitting needles stopped moving. One of them seemed to point right at me.

"I mean . . . ," I said, trying to think of a good word. One Mama would think acceptable. "She doesn't look too, uh, lean. She appears to have, um, meat on her." Grandmother Gallagher was beginning to sound a little like a chicken right before dinnertime.

Father smiled and glanced at Mama, his eyebrows raised a tiny bit.

At long last he said, "I think you'll be needing a private talk with your mother soon."

I watched Mama, who was now knitting furiously.

"Perhaps an interview with your youngest child, Flo," he continued.

"Of course," Mama said, keeping her head down.

Papa brought me close and whispered in my ear. "All good things come to those who wait," he said and sent me to bed with a kiss.

All good things come to those who wait. I thought about it over and over while I washed and changed for bed.

Did Father really mean *all* good things? I wondered as I began to fall asleep that evening. Truly? If so, I'd have more to wait for than just not being too skinny. I'd have to wait for Joshua. Once I wasn't feeling so angry with him, I mean.

Chapter Five

Talking to Joshua

Father worked in the fields early, almost before the sun was up, then headed off each morning for his store that was situated next to one of our town's two saloons.

Those saloons have caused a stir here in our community. I heard those words straight from Sister Barney's lips one afternoon when Mama went for a visit over at her home. She and Mama and two or three other ladies were meeting to talk about the evils of strong drink. They were quite boisterous* about this. The women, I mean. I know because I listened at the front window, sitting behind some thorny rose bushes. That was one time I did not get caught.

The saloons still stand, but that doesn't mean

Caroline's Secret

Mama doesn't cross to the other side of the street every time she comes for a visit with Father. And so do most other women, I've noticed. Cross the street, I mean. But I don't. I stay right on this sidewalk the whole way down. I think I'm braver because of my calling as a spy.

Being a spy takes good noticing and careful creeping about, too. I've done a great deal of studying of the two spy books that Father has in his store. That's how I know this. One of the books is called *Jesse Parker: Spy of the West* and the other is *Jesse Parker: Spy at the Capitol.* Jesse Parker has to be one of the most famous spies that's ever lived. He'd never make some of the mistakes I've made. I can truly testify that being caught in trees can be most embarrassing. And I have learned from my own experience that being apprehended* is not the choice a spy prefers. At least, I'm sure that Jesse Parker wouldn't want to be. Apprehended, I mean.

Monday morning early, I went to visit Father at his store. Sometimes I sweep the place out for him, or arrange the bolts of cloth, or dust the counters. That was my intention that morning—

to help Father and to practice walking without a sound.

This is not easy, walking without a sound. It takes a great deal of spy skill. Lucky for me, because it was summer and hot as fire, Mama didn't make me wear my shoes. It is much harder to walk quiet on wooden sidewalks if you have shoes on. Especially if they're pinching your toes.

My feet being free from confinement, I walked placing one foot in front of the other, much like an Indian might. I tried hard not to make the sidewalk squeak. I was concentrating so much that I almost ran straight into Joshua. At first, I smiled. Then I remembered what a traitor he was.

"Caroline," he said, stepping out of my way.

"Joshua," I said, and lifted my nose into the air at the sight of him. I said his name with such spite, one might think I had sworn.

"Where you off to?" he asked.

Now I lowered my nose and tried to look down it at him, but because Joshua is a good deal taller than me, I couldn't see him too well. Only his knees.

Caroline's Secret

"As if it's any of your business," I said in my most superior tone. I took a step to move forward, closer to my father's store.

Joshua stepped right in front of me. "Now, Caroline, you're not mad at me, are you?"

I raised my eyebrows the way I've seen both Mama and Father do. I raised them so high I actually felt my hairline go up in the front. "Brother Walker," I said. "I have an appointment to keep, so I best be on my way."

"But you're not wearing shoes," he said, pointing to my dust-covered feet. "No lady would keep an appointment without her shoes."

"Lady?" I said, my voice rising high. "I didn't think *you'd* call me a lady." I pointed at Joshua, feeling anger, embarrassment, and sadness fill up my throat. "I'm much too skinny and ugly for a lady." I marched around Joshua then. I didn't care if everybody in Farmington heard me. I stomped away loud and fast.

"Caroline, wait," Joshua said. He came to the side of me, stepping fast to keep up. "Now, I didn't know you heard what I said yesterday. I was just talking to your brother."

I didn't say anything but kept walking, getting closer to my father's store, where I planned to go into the storeroom in the back and cry in a pile of rags.

Joshua walked sideways, trying to catch my eye as we went. "I didn't know you were in that tree."

I stopped still and, with my hands on my hips, said, "So that's it. You don't say mean things to a person's face. Only when you think they're not around."

Joshua, who had overstepped me, came back to where I was. "Now that's not what I mean."

"Just what do you mean, Joshua Walker?" There were tears in my eyes. Tears of anger and hurt.

Joshua looked down at the sidewalk. When he spoke, his voice was barely above a whisper. "I was trying to find out about you, Caroline. You know, see how you were doing. I thought if I teased at your brother some, he'd tell me."

A horse and buggy moved down the street, followed by a wagon carrying a load of quarry stone.* *Somebody must be building a house*, I thought, watching the wagon go past. I waited, silent, weighing Joshua's words.

A true spy would know what to do with the boy, now that he seemed so humble. But I didn't. In fact, for a moment, he almost won me over. Then I remembered his dying scene after Peter said he thought maybe Joshua was sweet on me.

I narrowed my eyes. "A real friend," I said, poking Joshua in the shoulder with what I hoped was a knobby finger, "would never have said the words you spoke." And I flounced off down the sidewalk again.

This time Joshua did not follow. Instead, he said, in a voice that I almost didn't hear, "I'm real sorry, Caroline. I wasn't aiming to hurt you."

I slowed my step, then quickened it again. My pride gave me the strength to go on, and I almost felt good about it.

I made it all the way to Father's store before the tears came down my cheeks. These were tears that should have been cried the first time I heard Joshua's words, so when they came I didn't even have time to run into the back room.

"Caroline," said Marie. "Whatever is the matter?"

"Nothing," I shouted. Mama would have been unhappy about my not acting like a little lady. Especially since there were customers here. I felt glad she was still at home, working around the house, preparing for Father to come home for dinner.

I tried to make it to the storeroom, but I ran into Sister Rogers, our next-door neighbor, and a woman that I knew I had met before but whose name I couldn't remember.

"Careful, child," Sister Rogers said, and she steadied me with her hands gentle on my shoulders.

"Excuse me," I said, turning my face so she could not see my tears.

Sister Rogers bent close to me and, removing a handkerchief from her wrist, dabbed at my tears. The smell of lilacs drifted around my face, and for a moment I felt a little comforted. She looked me close in the eye, and I wondered if maybe she knew how much my heart hurt, but she never said a word about it if she did.

Instead, she smiled and, straightening, said, "Your father's in the back getting a few items for me." She turned to the woman near her and said, "I think this should complete all that we'll need for the meeting, Sister Eliza."

For a moment I was stunned. So stunned that even as a spy I was unable to move. It was like I had been frozen by Sister Rogers's words.

"Sister Eliza." I said the words under my breath, trying to remember and eyeing this woman as any good spy might. And then I knew who she was. Why, she wrote poetry. This woman was married to Brigham Young, the prophet.

A spy, I thought, *is not slow-witted. Not according to Father's books. A spy always knows what to do and then goes about it smoothly.* I moved into action. "Sister Eliza Snow," I said aloud.

Sister Snow, her hair white and pulled back from her face in a tight bun, nodded her head at me. Then she extended her hand.

"And who might you be?" she asked.

For a moment I could not remember who I

was, and then my memory blazed. "I'm Caroline Eyrely Gallagher. Able Gallagher, the proprietor of this store, is my father. I'm his youngest child. I'm almost fourteen, my birthday is coming this month, and I have done quite well in school. In fact, I have even been reading."

"The Good Book?" Sister Snow asked.

"A few very good books," I said. "The Book of Mormon, of course, and the Bible. But also some adventures. I've decided to become a well-known spy."

Sister Snow nodded as if perhaps she, too, had considered spying as a profession. "A well-known spy," she said. "And do you plan any other vocation?"*

I stopped for a moment to consider. If I said I wanted to be a writer, a poet even, Sister Snow might think well of me. I might even say I planned to marry a prophet. But neither was quite true.

"No ma'am," I said. "Just a spy."

Sister Rogers spoke up. "Sister Florence

Gallagher, Caroline's mother, will be meeting with us this afternoon, also."

"Perhaps we'll meet again then, Caroline," Sister Snow said.

"My pleasure," I said, sounding very grown-up, if I do say so myself.

"Caroline." My name floated in from outside.

I knew the voice that called me but I didn't want to look toward the door.

"Caroline."

"Excuse me," I said to Sister Rogers and Sister Snow. "I have a customer to wait on."

I turned and walked toward the front door of the store, where Joshua stood waiting.

"May I help you?" I asked in a voice loud enough for all to hear. In fact, people in the street may have even heard my words.

Joshua motioned to me with his hand. "Come here."

"I'm busy," I said and picked up a nearby horse bit and studied it as though I had come to make a purchase.

"Hurry," Joshua said.

Marie walked behind the counter until she

stood near the door and Joshua. "Aren't you Michael Walker's brother?" she asked.

He nodded.

"Won't you tell him Marie Gallagher said hello?"

Joshua nodded again, then whispered to me, "Hurry, Caroline."

My curiosity, and the look on Joshua's face, got the best of me then. I set down the horse bit and, with great dignity, rushed to the door.

Chapter Six

Wagon Ride

Outside Father's store, the sun was up pretty good. It shone down State Street, lighting things with a pure yellow color. To me, morning is a peaceful time of day.

Most times, that is. Now I stared Joshua Walker right in the eye, wondering what more he could say to hurt me to the very center of my being.

"Caroline, walk a ways with me," he said.

Marie stood at the screened-in door, suddenly, looking out at the two of us. It made me uncomfortable to see her there. Why did she have to listen in on my conversation? Was my whole family turning into spies?

"Just a ways, Joshua," I said. "Out of earshot."

I made sure I said this last bit loud and clear, for the listening-in ears. Then I looked back at Marie. She moved away from sight, but I could still feel her back there, watching.

We walked two doors down and sat on the sidewalk. Mama would be proud that I chose to go opposite of where the saloon is located.

"What is it you want?" I asked.

"I want you to forgive me, Caroline." Joshua looked down at his hands. "I've already told you why I did what I did. It was wrong of me."

"Why should I?"

"Because I said I was sorry. What more can I do to make you believe me? I followed you here this morning. I would have talked to you sooner, but your mama made it known she didn't want me too close on account of you-know-what."

"The fire," I said.

He nodded.

"But how can I know you're being truthful? I can't see into your heart. Maybe you're planning more mean words right now."

Joshua stared into my eyes so hard I had to look away. I swallowed and glanced up.

"You have to trust me, I guess."

I sat silent and thought. I was right, but so was he. I didn't know his heart, but if I didn't believe him, I might never sit with him like this again.

"I believe you," I said at long last.

Joshua let out a big breath and smiled. Then he and I sat quiet.

From way down the road I could see a wagon coming along slow-like, kicking up dust in the morning light.

A door squeaked open and slammed shut. Sister Rogers's voice reached me: "I've been giving it a lot of thought, as Brother Brigham asked. I think maybe I have come upon a solution."

"We can work out the details at our meeting this afternoon," Sister Snow said. Then the two women were past us and headed in the direction of Sister Rogers's home on Main Street.

"Here comes a wagon," Joshua said.

"Probably off for more quarry stone," I said.

Joshua looked at me sideways. "Catch a ride with me?"

"What?"

"Catch a ride on the back? It's not hard at all."

I looked at the wagon, rolling at a leisurely pace toward us. I'd never jumped on the back of one, though I knew of girls who had.

"We could ride it down to where I know some ripe peaches are."

"Peaches?" I said, like I'd never heard the word.

"Sure, come on." Joshua stood and dusted his hands on his pant legs.

Would a spy do something like this? I wondered. But I was already standing, already dusting my hands off, too.

"Run behind it and grab hold," Joshua said. "Then pull yourself up and sit in the bed. If it's really going out to the quarry, the wagon will take us right where we need to go."

The wagon didn't seem to be going so fast until I came up on it. I concentrated so hard on where I was supposed to climb aboard that I never even saw who drove or whether it was a horse or mule that pulled it along.

Joshua managed to run behind the wagon, with me trailing after him. He grabbed onto a wooden side, then leapt into place. It seemed to take him no effort at all.

But for me it was different.

I ran along okay, past where Sister Rogers and Sister Snow walked, my hand gripping at the wooden wagon rail that seemed to be made entirely from splinters.

"This hurts," I said.

"Jump on," Joshua said.

"I'm trying," I said. But the problem was that I couldn't seem to get up enough speed to jump. "The wagon keeps moving."

Joshua reached out for me and I grabbed onto his hand.

"On three I'll help pull you up. Kind of hop, but hop big," he said.

Hop big? I thought. But I never had a chance to say it.

"One, two, three."

I jumped a little, but because the wagon was moving I managed to do nothing but jump after it. Then I missed a step and tripped. I dragged a while, my toes scraping at the dusty road, one arm stretching its way to Joshua, before he was able to hoist part of me beside him.

Somehow I got a leg on the lip of the wagon bed. I hopped on one foot, at a quick pace, until Joshua was able to reach down and pull up my other leg. I very nearly flipped backwards, but I managed to flop into the back of the wagon. I lay there on my stomach, my legs kicking like I was swimming. Thank goodness Joshua had dragged me all the way onto the bed of prickly wood.

"Ouch," I said, out of breath and trying to turn myself into the sitting position. "Sure am glad I'm skinny and knobby. I think it saved my life."

"Are you hurt?" Joshua asked, ignoring my words.

That's when I saw Sister Rogers's face. Her eyes were as big as saucers. And Sister Snow's mouth had dropped open. They had witnessed the whole thing. All the hopping and all the swimming. I squeezed my eyes shut.

"Not hurt," I said, as we drove further and

further away from the Prophet Brigham Young's wife. "A little embarrassed."

"Next time it won't be so hard," Joshua said.

Next time, I thought. I couldn't see there'd be a next time, not with Mama being such good friends with Sister Rogers. And what had Sister Snow said? Something about working out details? Something about Mama meeting with those two? I dropped my head into my hands. I was going to be in trouble.

I'd like to say that the sweet taste of peaches made the troubled feeling in my heart go away, but of course that wouldn't be true. They just made the awful worry climb far enough back into my head that I only noticed it every once in a while.

Being with Joshua, the peaches, and the long walk back into town kind of dimmed my mind as to what might be happening. What might be waiting for me. I could only hope that Sister Snow didn't feel like writing any poetry about what she had seen me do. I'd heard once that she took the inspiration of life to get her ideas. I hoped I hadn't been helpful to her.

He was so nice, Joshua was, that I decided right then and there, on our walk, to forgive him for sure and without a doubt for all the things he had said before and probably a few things he might even say in the future. I let him make the trek back with me, carrying the peaches he had chosen as a gift for Mama. If it hadn't been for the awful nagging feeling that whispered over and over again in my head, I think I'd have been fine, maybe even happier than I'd ever been before.

It was when we went past Sister Rogers's house that I remembered the meeting. I could see there were a few carriages near the front of her yard.

It hit me then, just like I bet it would have hit Jesse Parker, that I knew which room was the meeting room. I knew which window to listen under.

"Joshua," I said, interrupting his talk about his father's furniture carving and all the chores the boys in his family had to do. "I have some spy business to go about. I best be at my duty."

Joshua's eyes grew large. "Spy?" he asked.

I bowed my head and smiled. "Yes, spy. I've decided I want to make that my life's work."

"And who do you plan to spy on?"

"If I told you," I said, "that wouldn't make me a very responsible spy. They have to be quiet and not spread around what they're doing. They keep secrets."

"Then why did you say anything about it, Caroline? Did you secretly want me to go with you? To be your partner, maybe?" Joshua grinned so big I noticed a little peach skin stuck in his back teeth.

"Partner?" I asked, my voice sounding squeaky like an old wheel. I thought about it a minute. Every partner Jesse Parker ever had got killed. I sure didn't want that happening to Joshua. So I changed things around a bit. "Every partner I've ever known about has gotten killed," I said. "This is dangerous work."

"Killed?"

"Dead." I rolled my eyes back into my head and tried to look as dead as I could in the standing position.

Joshua came close to me and laid his hand on my arm. His palm was just a little sticky from the peaches, and dirty, too, but I didn't care. "I wouldn't get killed," he said. "In fact, I might be able to save you in a pinch. Let me work with you, Caroline."

I'm not sure what made me change my mind. It could have been the sweet stickiness of the peaches, or Joshua's smile, or the way he seemed to look right into my head and know my thoughts. But right at that moment, in the heat of the day with the sun pounding down on us and a slight breeze blowing over Main Street, I made the decision to take on a partner: Joshua Walker.

Chapter Seven

Caught... Again

Mama caught me and Joshua sitting under Sister Rogers's window only after I had heard three things: that children needed to be guided a little better, that boys were to be counseled to not steal fruit from the gardens of others, and that girls should not jump on the back of wagons, as it could be dangerous.

I glanced over at Joshua after I heard Sister Rogers mention girls and wagons. He looked like he had borrowed his eyes from a grasshopper, they were that buggy. I tried to smile at him some, but my mouth wouldn't work at all. That's when I noticed Mama. She was taking big steps to where the two of us crouched amongst the white daisies and purple coneflowers, and she didn't even look a little bit happy. I noticed her dark dress was flapping in the wind. I hoped she didn't see us. Maybe we had blended into the flowers.

"What are the two of you doing?" Mama screeched.

"She's seen us," I said.

Joshua said nothing.

"I said, what are the two of you doing?" I could tell right then and there I was never going to make it to the safety of the parlor as Peter had. I could also tell that I would be blessed if I made it off Sister Rogers's property with just an ear pulling like Joshua was getting at that very moment. I could tell I was gonna be blessed if I lived more than a minute or two longer.

I guess, as a spy, I don't really need to mention that Mama never made it to the meeting herself. She was coming over late, which she told Father later was heaven-sent, because she had been helping Marie calm down. It seems Michael Walker had visited Father at the store and asked for permission to court her. Marie, I mean.

Marie had been so excited when Father said

yes that she ran herself nearly the whole way home and told Mama. Mama was late to the meeting for listening to all the details and to how Marie really did favor Michael to all the other young men in Farmington.

"That's when," Mama said, telling Father the whole ugly story the way she thought it should go, "I saw the two of them." She pointed at me and an imaginary Joshua Walker. Joshua was already home. And hadn't he said he'd save me in a pinch? This was at least a pinch, or even a whole grab, and where was he? Gone! And I was all alone at the store with only Father and Mama. She'd locked the door behind her so no customers would enter. Who would dare? I wondered. No one, if they heard the fire in her words.

"There they were, sitting in her flowers." Mama leaned close to Father, expressing her unhappiness not only with her voice but with her face and her body as well. Even Father seemed to tremble from fear. At least, I think that's why he was shaking.

"I was horrified, Able. Our daughter was listening in on an important meeting. A meeting that Bishop Hess has already spoken to us about. To think of the unruliness of some children!"

Mama turned right around and looked at me, sitting on the pickle barrel. I lowered my eyes, feeling ashamed. This spying occupation didn't seem to be working out for me, not in the least bit. Every time I tried to do it right, I failed miserably. Perhaps I needed to study Father's books a bit harder. Perhaps there was a special school I could go to. Perhaps . . .

"Caroline!" Mama's voice nearly took off my skin.

"Yes, ma'am?"

"Your father asked you a question."

"Yes, sir?"

"I asked you, Daughter, if you and I need a little time to talk this over?"

I wasn't quite sure what to answer. Did he want me to talk to him or not? I looked into my own self for the answer. *I* wanted to talk to him. I nodded, closing my eyes.

"I don't want her talking to that Joshua Walker boy for a while. There's a chance I might faint if I knew what the two of them had been about."

I didn't argue. It would have done no good to. I did make sure I didn't look at Mama then. I had a pretty strong feeling she wouldn't like the idea of me in the back of a wagon.

"See that she is dealt a severe punishment, Able," Mama said. "I'm off to find out what I missed from a meeting I should have been a part of." And then she *was* off, stomping down the sidewalk, alerting people before her and behind her that she was either coming or had just been there.

I kept my head down until Father called my name again.

"Caroline, whatever has inspired you to do all this eavesdropping? I'm not angry with you. I just need to see into the heart of my youngest child."

"Oh, Father," I said. I jumped off the pickle barrel and ran to him. Throwing my arms around his waist, I hugged him as hard as I could. And I told him everything, tears running down my cheeks as I spoke.

I told him of Jesse Parker and the exciting life

he led, about my own dream to be a spy, about Marie being soft and round and me being knobby. I told him about Joshua and his harsh words and then his kind words. Everything bubbled out of me till there was nothing left to do but beg forgiveness from him.

"Forgiveness from a parent is an easy thing to ask," Father said. "I think you'll be needing to talk to Sister Rogers and Sister Snow. It was them whose confidence you interfered with."

I closed my eyes and drew in a deep breath. Father was right. But I didn't know if I had the courage to do what he said needed to be done.

"It's time for supper, Caroline," Father said. "I'll walk over with you now. You can clear this up right away. Then it won't seem so bad."

I bowed my head again, tears filling my eyes. "If you're with me, Father, I think I'd have the courage to talk to the prophet himself."

Father closed up shop and, taking steps as small as I could, I walked the path any spy would hate. The path toward confession.

Father took my hand. "Now there is something that I think you need to understand."

"What, Father?"

It was early evening now. Supper, I knew, would be waiting for Father and me.

A night bird sang, and a cat ran along the sidewalk. The air was still warm, and a breeze had picked up and was blowing in from the canyon.

"There is no Jesse Parker."

I stopped in my tracks. "What?"

"There is no spy called Jesse Parker. He's a character in somebody's story. There really isn't a man going about peeping into other people's lives and not getting caught. I thought you should know."

"No Jesse Parker?" I didn't even know if it was worth trying to breathe right then.

Father rubbed my head with his hand, and the touch told me he loved me and didn't want me to feel too sad.

I started walking. In no time, in too soon a time, we were at Sister Rogers's door.

I knocked so softly that Father had to knock after me.

Brother Rogers opened the door and let Father and me in the house.

"May I see Sister Rogers?" I asked, and my voice was so small no one but Brother Rogers could have heard it.

"Aurelia, you have a guest in the front hall." Brother Rogers's voice echoed around me and for a moment I wondered if everyone in my whole town didn't know I was here in this home.

"Oh, Caroline," Sister Rogers said when she came into the hall and saw me there. "I was hoping you might come by."

Father excused himself and went to stand with Brother Rogers in front of the house.

"Ma'am," I said. I had to get it over with, so without hesitating I blurted everything out. "I'm real sorry about what I did this afternoon. I wasn't meaning to cause harm. I was only interested in knowing if Mama would find out about me on the back of the wagon with Joshua. Please, won't you forgive me?"

Sister Rogers looked me over and then, gesturing toward a chair, asked me to sit. I did.

"I need to tell you of a good friend of mine, Caroline, from many years ago. I knew her after my mother died, when we left Nauvoo. This girl, this Catherine from so long ago, reminds me of you. She was a bit of a spy, too. She told me plenty of stories about her own listening."

Sister Rogers smiled at her memory. Then she looked back at me. "It wasn't right of her then to listen to private things, just as it's not right for you now. But Catherine managed to grow into a magnificent woman, and I'm sure you will too. If you do the right things."

"Did she stay a spy?"

"No, not that I know. She did have five boys. And she died not too long ago."

"Oh." I ducked my head, saddened a little by the fact that Catherine had not made it as a spy. Sad, too, that I wouldn't, either.

Sister Rogers stood, letting me know I could leave. "We'll be needing some good singers in our new children's organization, Caroline. Do you think you could make it?"

"Yes, I think so," I said. But my heart didn't mean my answer. It was still trying to give up the idea of keeping secrets.

CHAPTER EIGHT

The First Meeting for Children

Sunday, August 25, was the day of the new meeting for children here in our little town. To keep us busy, I suppose. Or off the backs of wagons.

It was hot when we met in Rock Chapel. It seemed about a million children were there, but I knew that couldn't be, because there are just over two hundred children in our town. According to Father, that is.

I moved my way around the room, trying to find someone to sit with other than Peter and looking for Joshua out of the corner of my eye. I saw a few girls from school but decided to sit alone and just watch and wait.

Joshua hadn't been by to see Peter or me for the whole of two weeks. I had missed him  plenty, especially with Marie always stumbling about the house saying things like "That Michael Walker is a good fellow." And, "That Michael Walker surely is kind to the widows in our town." I had felt good and sick of Michael Walker until two evenings before when he came for a visit.

"Caroline," he said when Marie had settled him in the parlor and had run into the kitchen to bring him out some cake she'd made for him. "I've a message for you."

"What?" I asked. "A message? Who would send me a message?" But I knew. My heart started pounding.

Michael motioned to me with his finger, and I came toward him. In a light voice he whispered, "'Tell Caroline to save me a place at the meeting on Sunday,' my brother said. 'Tell Caroline that I hope we're still partners.'"

"Still partners," I said, my voice as soft as Michael's, just as secret.

"Are you?" Michael asked.

I didn't have time to answer because Marie came in with the cake, thick and sugary, on a small flowered plate. One of Mama's good plates.

But Michael waited for my answer. "Well?" he asked.

"Yes," I said, my face turning red as the strawberries that decorated the fine white cake. "Tell him I said yes."

It was then and there that I decided that Michael Walker was not only good to the widows of the town but also good to the lonely.

Now, sitting on the hard bench, I remembered the message for the millionth time and waited. Someone called the meeting to order and then someone else said the prayer. We were reminded that Sister Aurelia Rogers was the new president of the Primary Mutual Improvement Association of The Church of Jesus Christ of Latter-day Saints. Bishop Hess spoke about how we were in attendance at the very first meeting of this sort—and that's when I saw Joshua. He was across the chapel from me, near one of the windows. He looked uncomfortable in his Sunday best, and I didn't blame him at all. The day was a sweltering one.

His eyes met mine and he nodded his head a slight bit and started to make his way over to me. Before he had gone too far, Sister Wells stood up and addressed us. She divided us into groups by age.

Joshua was moved to the bench right behind me then, being that we are just a year apart in age. When no one was looking, he leaned over and slipped me a tiny piece of paper with a note on it. It said, "Meet you in your tree after church?"

For a while I couldn't catch his eye, not with all the shuffling going on, but then at last I did. I nodded to him and he smiled an answer back.

The meeting couldn't get over too soon for me. Another secret! All I could think of was getting home, even though some of what the leaders talked about sounded exciting: annual fairs, home arts, and gardening projects were just a few of the things planned for us to do.

Sister Rogers stood then and spoke. "I'm here to give you a bit of counsel," she said. "Young men, it is wrong to take fruits and melons from the fields of other people. And girls, it is not ladylike to catch a ride on the back of a wagon. It is also dangerous. And finally, remember to be obedient to your parents."

I didn't care to hear any of this. It was far too embarrassing. I glanced around to see if anyone noticed that Sister Rogers was speaking to me. No one seemed to, though I did get a bit of a poke between my shoulder blades. Only Joshua knew.

I wanted this meeting to end so I could get home and climb my tree. Two weeks had been a long enough separation from Joshua, I was sure.

And Father was not home again. He had left this morning. Oh, how I would miss him, but I could not bother him so soon at Sister Elizabeth's.

At last the meeting was out. I started from the building, hurrying to get home so I could change from this hot Sabbath-day dress to one a little cooler.

Peter came up alongside me. He fingered the neckline of his collar. "I'm awful glad we won't have any more of these meetings on Sunday," he said. "Saturdays we won't have to be dressed so formal."

Joshua and a few of his younger brothers joined us, and it seemed my heart missed a beat. My cheeks pinkened and I wondered if anyone saw.

"I've heard, though," Joshua said, "that we'll be wearing uniforms."

"Everyone?" I asked.

"I've heard just the boys," he said.

Peter groaned. "Isn't that the way it always is? Girls have the easiest lives."

"Unless they're caught on the back of a wagon," Joshua said, and he looked hard into my face and broke out into a grin.

We were home then. Before I could go inside, Joshua grabbed my hand in his. His skin was dry and warm. My heart missed a beat. "After dinner?" he whispered.

I nodded.

"Look," a younger brother cried. "He's holding onto her like Michael does with his girl."

Joshua dropped my hand and moved away. "So you've been spying on them, have you, Aaron?" And the group left, Joshua teasing his brothers as they went.

I turned to go into the house and there was Peter smiling so wide that I thought his face might snap into parts. "So there are two beaus for the Gallagher girls," he said. "And they're both the Walkers."

"Excuse me," I said, pushing past him. I went in to help Mama with the next meal, a smile tugging at the sides of my mouth . . . and tugging at my heart, too.

CHAPTER NINE

A Secret for My Heart Only

If I checked the tree once I checked it a thousand times, especially after dinner. In and out of the house I ran until Mama finally said, "Caroline, your slamming that door is like the pounding of a hammer against my temples. And you're letting in flies. Stay inside, or go out, but make up your mind."

I could see that she was already missing Father, though he had been gone but a few hours.

Since I had just come from outside, I decided to stay in a while. I went to the room I shared with Marie. She sat on the edge of the bed, her hands folded in her lap.

"Excuse me," I said. "I didn't know you were

here." I wanted to go to the window because I knew if I could look out the back I might see Joshua.

Marie smiled a little then said, "Have you ever thought of me marrying?"

I looked at her. Had I? I shook my head.

"I think I will," she said. "Marry Michael Walker. He hasn't asked Father yet, but *we* have spoken of things."

I came and sat next to her on the bed, forgetting Joshua for the moment. "What kinds of things?" I asked, but Marie only smiled at me.

"Secret things?" I asked, but she only smiled.

"I'll miss you, Caroline," she said after a minute. "We've always been such good friends, and it will be hard not to have you near."

A lump came up in my throat all of a sudden. "You are planning to leave, aren't you?"

She nodded.

"But we'd still be close. I mean, wouldn't you stay here in Farmington?"

"I'd go where Michael went."

"I'd think he'd stay close," I said. "His family has been here since the settling of this area."

Caroline's Secret

Marie and I sat on the bed, quiet and close for a long while, until the sun began to sink far away and I remembered Joshua. I peeked out the window but could not see him—in the tree or anywhere near.

I made my way downstairs, past Mama knitting in the parlor, past Peter eating a piece of pie in the kitchen, and on out into the back. A cool breeze blew the warmth of the day far away from me, causing the limbs of the pine I had hidden in to sway. I went to the bottom branches of the tree and looked up. Joshua sat near the top. No wonder I hadn't seen him.

"You're late," he said but made no move to climb down.

"Should I follow you up?" I asked, and without waiting for an answer I started the climb, my hands grasping the rough bark of the tree limbs.

"You've heard, haven't you?" he asked when I sat on a branch opposite him.

"About Marie and Michael?" I asked.

He shook his head. "That we're leaving. My family will be gone by the end of the summer.

Father has been asked to come into Salt Lake and start his furniture building there."

"What?" I asked. The words had trouble making their way to my head. "Leaving?"

Joshua nodded at me, then took in a deep breath. "And you're right, too, about Michael. I think he'll ask your sister to go along."

Would Marie go? Would she leave us to live with Michael? I knew in a moment that she would. Salt Lake is only fifteen miles away, she would say. And I could tell by looking at her face when Michael was near how she felt about him.

"And you're going, too?" I asked.

"Yes," he said. His simple answer, though I had expected none other, seemed to cut me to the bone. I closed my eyes against tears. All along I had wanted to know secrets and I knew them, before anyone in my family, perhaps. But they were painful and hard, like thorns.

Joshua began to make his way down the tree, and I followed. "We could see each other again if you wanted, Caroline Gallagher. I'd like to always be your friend. I'd like," he took another deep breath, "to be more than a friend."

Caroline's Secret

Another secret, one for my heart, grew from Joshua's words.

"I just want you to remember me. Do you think you will?"

"Yes, Joshua," I said. "How could I forget the fellow who helped me into my first wagon?" Any other time my words might have been funny. But they were not now. In fact, they were binding words, somehow linking Joshua and me together until the next time I should meet with him.

We sat in the tree until the sun sank low behind the hills and Mama missed me. We talked seldom. Mostly I thought of Joshua close by and wondered if he thought like I did. Was his heart full of secrets like mine? Would my sister go with his family when they left? Would he miss me?

When the night birds sang, Mama called me in.

I left Joshua in the tree with a quiet good-bye. All the way into the house, through the dark yard toward the light in the doorway, I remembered Father's words, "All good things come to those who wait." I thought of my own heart and a secret that grew there. And knew I would never forget.

GLOSSARY
In Caroline's Own Words

apprehended—To be apprehended is to be arrested or caught. Not good for a spy's career! See page 42.

boisterous—Mama often calls my brother boisterous—meaning loud and noisy. But as a spy I have learned that Mama and the other ladies can also be quite boisterous when they get together for ladies' meetings. See page 41.

conclusion—Part of a spy's work is watching people's actions and listening to them talk in order to reach a *conclusion*. In plain English that means to figure something out. See page 22.

Deseret—The area of Deseret is what later became the state of Utah. It was a big area of land, but it was whittled down until it's the size you know today. See page 14.

Farmington—A pioneer settlement fifteen miles north of Salt Lake City, Utah. See page 24.

gall—When I said Peter had gall, I meant he had a lot of nerve to be telling Father those things about me. Brothers! See page 26.

girth—When I said that Peter spoke into Mama's girth, I

Glossary

meant Mama is a big woman. Girth is the distance around something. See page 16.

gyrating—Joshua's gyrating around meant that he was doing a crazy, jerking dance on the ground. Boys can be like that. See page 6.

perplexed—Peter looked perplexed when Mama was giving him a lecture. That means he looked worried. See page 14.

quarry stone—People will go to the same place, a pit that is called a quarry, to gather good building stones. Chimneys, fireplaces, and sometimes parts of houses are built of quarry stone. See page 45.

settee—A settee is a small sofa. Ours traveled with us from Michigan. See page 37.

simpered—When Peter and Joshua simpered, it meant they smiled like they hadn't done anything wrong. See page 9.

vocation—When Sister Snow was asking me what my vocation might be, she wondered what I planned on doing as a career. Mostly women are wives and mothers in the nineteenth century, but sometimes they become famous poets like Sister Snow. See page 49.

What Really Happened

Aurelia Rogers was concerned for the welfare of the children in Farmington, Utah. She worried about the disobedience of boys. They stole fruit from trees that did not belong to them and stole melons from other people's gardens. Many boys stayed out late at night. Sister Rogers even thought some of the older boys were acting like hoodlums. After President Brigham Young's visit to Farmington in 1877, Sister Rogers thought a great deal about what should happen to help guide the children in God's true church. Her chief worry was, If the boys were not taught and trained well, then who would the young girls marry? Something had to be done.

At last she came upon the idea of an organization for young boys that could help them become good men. She discussed the idea with Eliza R. Snow, Relief Society general president. Shortly thereafter, President John Taylor, Brigham

Young's successor as president of the Church, approved the plan for a children's organization.

On August 11, 1878, the Farmington Ward Primary Association was organized. The first meeting was held on Sunday, August 25. Sister Aurelia Spencer Rogers was called as the first president of this organization.

In the beginning it was thought to be an organization just for boys, but then it was decided that good singing voices would be needed, so girls were invited to attend as well.

Regular meetings were held on Saturday afternoons, and children participated in lots of fun things. They entered gardening contests, learned lessons on gospel principles, and even had annual fairs.

About the Author

No wonder Carol Lynch Williams enjoys writing books for girls—she's surrounded by them! After having grown up with a sister and her grandmother, Carol married and had four daughters of her own. She is expecting a fifth baby.

Carol grew up in Florida and joined the LDS Church when she was seventeen. She served a full-time LDS mission to deaf people in North Carolina and then moved to Utah, where she attended BYU, worked as an interpreter for the deaf, and began writing books. She and her family live in Mapleton, Utah. Carol teaches Relief Society and is Achievement Day leader in her ward Primary, and she serves as assistant editor for the stake newsletter.

Carol's husband, Drew, writes, "Carol fills her family's life with her youthful sense of humor, great storytelling, and the yummiest bread a mom can bake!"

Carol has written five nationally published novels and six LDS novels. Earlier Latter-day Daughters books include *Sarah's Quest, Anna's Gift, Esther's Celebration, Marciea's Melody, Laurel's Flight,* and *Catherine's Remembrance.*

From *Janey's Own*
Another Exciting New Title
in the Latter-day Daughters Series

"We have heard," my Uncle Carl said, "though I'm certain it was a misunderstanding, that your papa is getting mixed up with those Mormons."

He leaned forward and looked straight at me—hard.

"Some folks in town," he said, "tell us that he has actually *become* one of them. They say that not too long ago, he abandoned you all here and has gone to join with them."

I wanted to slap his face. But I'm certainly not that brave.

"He didn't abandon us . . ." I stammered.

"Perhaps you don't realize the danger your father could be in."

"What danger?" I said.

"This country is full of marauders. They rob and kill people every day. And they don't like Mormons. Why, a man was found dead just last week on the road to Iowa."

I gasped without meaning to.